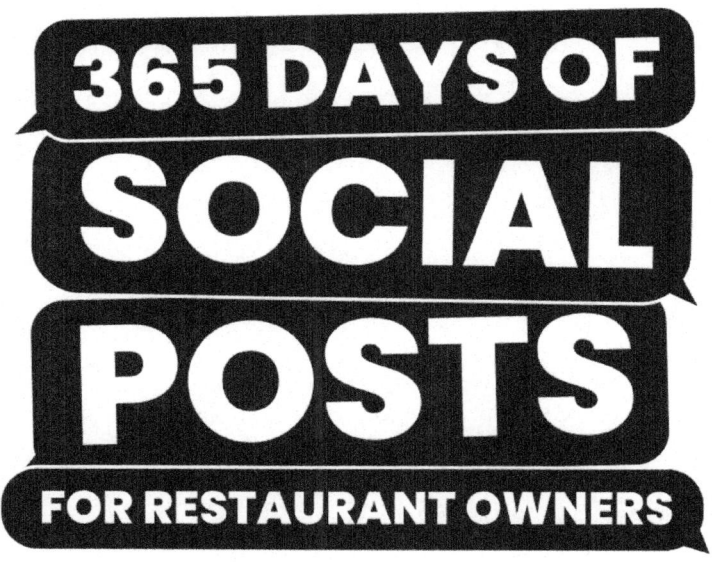

THE ULTIMATE GUIDE TO RESTAURANT SOCIAL MEDIA MARKETING

Brendan Cox

Copyright © 2021 Brendan Cox

All rights reserved.

DEDICATION

To you, the restaurant owner.

TABLE OF CONTENTS

January	1
February	32
March	60
April	91
May	121
June	152
July	182
August	213
September	246
October	278
November	310
December	342

ACKNOWLEDGMENTS

I would like to thank every one of you that has made my dream a reality. Whether you are a friend, family member, employee or simply a follower, thank you. You have fueled my social media journey over the years and without your support, none of what I have accomplished would've been possible.

Digital Assets

Claim Your **FREE** $20 Gift Card

 | Digital Products Online Store

Go to: 365DaysOfSocialPosts.com/go

365 Days of Social Posts for Restaurant Owners

JANUARY 1ST

New Year's Day

Caption: Happy New Year! Here's a look at some of our favorite dishes that were most memorable this year. Cheers to a new year, new goals, and delicious food!

—

Wish your followers a Happy New Year! Get creative and post pictures of your favorite food from this year.

JANUARY 2ND

New Year's Resolutions

Caption: Some people say New Year's resolutions are cliché, but they can be a great way to start fresh and accomplish goals you have been pushing off. This year I hope we hope to [insert your restaurants New Year's resolution here]. What are some of your goals for this year?

-

As a business owner, it's important to connect on a more personal level with potential customers. This is also a great way to get your followers to engage with your content.

JANUARY 3RD

Featured Special of The Week

Do This: Every week showcase your featured special of the week alongside a mouth-watering photo of the dish.

—

Use this as an opportunity to showcase a popular dish that you are proud of and emphasize that it is only available this week to encourage your followers to come try it.

JANUARY 4TH

National Trivia Day

Caption: It's National Trivia Day! The first person to answer correctly will win a [prize ideas: gift card, free dessert, or just do it for fun]. Example: We opened our doors in what year?

—

Remember, your social media can't be all pictures of food. In order to build a stronger relationship with your customers, it's important to post interesting content that encourages people to engage.

JANUARY 5TH

Highlighting a Review

Caption: Thank you for your kind words [Name of customer who shared the review]! Incredibly thankful for reviews like this.

—

Reviews are arguably the most important part of a successful restaurant. Make sure to share and showcase those hard-earned stars across your social media platforms. Not only will this entice potential clients, but it will encourage previous clients to also leave kind remarks.

JANUARY 6TH

Employee of The Month

Do This: Every month, recognize and profile one of your hard-working employees as "the employee of the month"

—

Although you may not initially think this is an impactful idea, customers love to get to know your staff. Showing your appreciation for your employees is also a great way to keep them motivated at work.

JANUARY 7TH

Restaurant History

Caption: Share a brief history of your restaurant and explain how and why you got started!

—

Believe it or not, people love to know the story behind a restaurant. Share how you got started in the food industry.

JANUARY 8TH

Team Appreciation

Caption: In the spirit of the new year, we wanted to take the time to recognize our team and give them a shout out for everything that they do! Every member of our team works incredibly hard, day in and day out to cater to all our amazing customers.

-

It is so important to take the time to recognize those around you.

JANUARY 9TH

Share a Recipe

Do This: Share a recipe of one of your dishes with your audience!

—

Contrary to popular belief, sharing recipes for some of your dishes does not diminish your brand value. Recipes deepen the bond between your food and your clientele and prove your expertise even more.

JANUARY 10TH

Featured Special of The Week

Do This: Every week showcase your featured special of the week alongside a mouth-watering photo of the dish.

—

Use this as an opportunity to showcase a popular dish that you are proud of and emphasize that it is only available this week to encourage your followers to come try it.

JANUARY 11TH

Staff Picks!

Do This: Share some of your staff's favorite dishes. Post a photo of them and their favorite menu-item along with a short description of why it's their go-to.

-

Customers always ask their waiters for recommendations, and this is a fun way to do something similar online!

JANUARY 12TH

Quote

Share This: "Good food is the foundation of genuine happiness."
- Auguste Escoffier

—

Creative use of a quote can help you drive more engagement and shares towards your restaurant. Branding relevant quotes with your logo on them will help expand your digital footprint.

JANUARY 13TH

Value Through Video

Do This: Create a video of you inside your kitchen showcasing one of your cooks making a popular dish or plating food!

–

Videos are becoming a more and more prominent and accessible way to digest information through social media.

JANUARY 14TH

Let's Talk

Do This: Create a poll or open-ended question asking your followers what new additions they would like to see added to your menu.

—

Use this post as a forum where your followers can comment or vote on new additions to your menu. Connecting with your audience is key and shows that you care and appreciate your customers.

JANUARY 15TH

Advertise an Appetizer

Caption: Let's be real, our appetizers are way underrated! Have you tried our [title of your dish]?

—

Appetizers never get enough social buzz! Use this as an opportunity to showcase your most popular appetizer!

JANUARY 16TH

Share Why You Are Unique

Do This: Explain what's unique about your restaurant.

—

Whether this relates to your secret recipe or your stunning location emphasize what makes your restaurant so unique.

JANUARY 17TH

Featured Special of The Week

Do This: Every week showcase your featured special of the week alongside a mouth-watering photo of the dish.

—

Use this as an opportunity to showcase a popular dish that you are proud of and emphasize that it is only available this week to encourage your followers to come try it.

JANUARY 18TH

Support Your Community

Do This: Get involved in a local fundraiser and offer to donate a portion of sales when customers mention the cause on their bill!

–

Getting involved in your community is extremely important as a restaurant. If you support your community, your community will support you.

JANUARY 19TH

Share a Customers Photo

Do This: Share a customer's photo that they posted on social media. Make sure to tag them and show your appreciation for them sharing their meal with the internet!

—

Word of mouth is the most powerful marketing tool. Sharing other customer photos will encourage others to share their photos online!

JANUARY 20TH

Showcase Some Behind the Scenes Content

Do This: Share a photo or a video showcasing the behind the scenes of your restaurant.

—

Whether this is showing your employees getting ready for a busy night or your chef preparing the food, social media loves to see the BTS.

JANUARY 21ST

Contest

Caption: Thought it would be a great idea for you and your friends to get in on the fun! Follow us [@username] and tag 3 friends below for a chance to win a $XX gift card to [insert restaurant name here]. We'll be choosing one winner randomly next week!

–

Contests are a great way to spread the word about your business by getting your followers to tag their friends.

JANUARY 22ND

Showcase a Dessert

Do This: Post a photo of one of your most popular dessert's.

—

Simply glancing at a photo of a mouth-watering dessert is enough to get many people to book a reservation! (Including myself)

JANUARY 23RD

Music Playlist

Caption: Some of you have expressed your love for the music we play in our restaurant. We wanted to share our Spotify® playlist with you so you can feel like you are at [name of restaurant] at home.

–

This is a fun and engaging post to share your music playlist to all your followers!

JANUARY 24TH

Featured Special of The Week

Do This: Every week showcase your featured special of the week alongside a mouth-watering photo of the dish.

—

Use this as an opportunity to showcase a popular dish that you are proud of and emphasize that it is only available this week to encourage your followers to come try it.

JANUARY 25TH

Community Events

Do This: Create a post sharing some upcoming events in your town. Get involved when possible!

—

Most towns have a town calendar that you can pull events from. Getting involved and showing your support for your community is crucial to becoming a successful restaurant.

JANUARY 26TH

National Spouses Day

Caption: Happy National Spouses Day. Today is a day to celebrate the bond between two people and show how much they are loved, respected, and appreciated.

-

Today is a great day to thank your significant other for being who they are! This is another excellent way to connect with your audience on a more personal level.

JANUARY 27TH

Featured Drink

Caption: We've got some delicious, featured drinks going this month. Check out our [describe drink here].

—

Whether it's a wine, coffee, or an over-the-top milkshake, share a drink that everyone has been loving!

JANUARY 28TH

Fun at Work Day

Caption: Did you know that it's Fun at Work Day? But let's be honest—every day is fun at work when you're satisfying taste buds for a living!

-

Today is an excellent opportunity to show that you are passionate about your job!

JANUARY 29TH

Restaurant Game

Do This: Create a chart that has 3 different combinations of a starter, entree and dessert and have your followers choose which 3-course meal they'd go with!

–

Who knows maybe they'll stop by and give one of these combo's a shot!

JANUARY 30TH

Fun Fact

Do This: Share a fun fact about your restaurant that most locals don't know about!

—

Lighten the mood with a surprising fact about your restaurant.

JANUARY 31ST

Food Photo of The Month

Caption: Introducing the January Food Photo of The Month! This amazing photo was taken by our lovely customer [insert name here] and features our signature [insert dish here].

–

The last day of the month is a great time to feature a beautiful photo taken by one of your customers!

FEBRUARY 1ST

Take Out Special

Do This: Offer an exclusive take out special for those who follow you on social media!

–

Use this as an opportunity to showcase some of the perks of following you on social media!

FEBRUARY 2ND

Groundhog Day

Caption: It's Groundhog Day! Are you rooting for 6 more weeks of winter or an early spring?

—

Remember, not everything has to relate back to food. Holidays are often a relatable subject that allow your followers to engage with you.

FEBRUARY 3ᴿᴰ

Featured Special of The Week

Do This: Every week showcase your featured special of the week alongside a mouth-watering photo of the dish.

—

Use this as an opportunity to showcase a popular dish that you are proud of and emphasize that it is only available this week to encourage your followers to come try it.

FEBRUARY 4TH

Thank a Mail Carrier Day

Caption: Today is National Thank a Mail Carrier Day! I wanted to do something special for our mail carrier, [insert name here], for all [his/her] hard work, day in and day out!

–

February 4th is a great day to do a kind deed along with showing your appreciation for your local mail carrier.

FEBRUARY 5TH

Quote

Share This: "Good food is good mood."

–

Share this foodie quote with your audience. Bonus points if you create a branded graphic with your logo on it rather than just sharing one off Google!

FEBRUARY 6TH

Highlighting a Review

Caption: Thank you for your 5-star review [Name of customer who shared the review]! We appreciate you dining with us!

–

Reviews are arguably the most important part of a successful restaurant. Make sure to share and showcase those hard-earned stars across your social media platforms. Not only will this entice potential clients, but it will encourage previous clients to also leave kind remarks.

FEBRUARY 7TH

Employee of The Month

Do This: Every month, recognize and profile one of your hard-working employees as "the employee of the month"

—

Although you may not initially think this is an impactful idea, customers love to get to know your staff. Showing your appreciation for your employees is also a great way to keep them motivated at work.

FEBRUARY 8TH

Did You Know...

Caption: Did you know we have a [insert name of dish]? [Describe the dish here]

–

Sometimes some of your underrated dishes are only underrated because people don't know about them!

FEBRUARY 9TH

National Pizza Day

Caption: Happy National Pizza Day! [insert name of pizza place] is hands down my favorite pizza place in town but I always love trying out new places. What's your go-to local pizzeria?

–

Showcase your love for your community by highlighting your favorite local pizzeria! (Or if you sell pizza at your establishment – showcase your pizza!)

FEBRUARY 10TH

Signature Dish

Do This: Showcase a heavenly photo of one of your signature dishes!

–

In the restaurant business – the quality of your photos of social media goes a long way. Make sure to study up on some camera tips or hire a professional photographer to shoot your food.

FEBRUARY 11TH

Featured Special of The Week

Do This: Every week showcase your featured special of the week alongside a mouth-watering photo of the dish.

–

Use this as an opportunity to showcase a popular dish that you are proud of and emphasize that it is only available this week to encourage your followers to come try it.

FEBRUARY 12TH

Valentine's Day Reservations

Do This: Encourage people to spend their Valentine's Day at your restaurant!

—

If you are offering a prefix menu or any Valentine's Day specials, make sure to let everyone know!

FEBRUARY 13TH

Packed House!

Do This: Showcase a photo of happy diners eating at your restaurant.

—

Someone once said, "a busy restaurant is a good restaurant." Emphasize this on social media.

FEBRUARY 14TH

Valentine's Day

Do this: Wish everyone a happy Valentine's Day along with sharing a special menu or prefix!

—

Valentine's Day is celebrated annually on February 14.

FEBRUARY 15TH

Free Birthday Dessert

Caption: Know someone celebrating a birthday this month? Get a dessert on us when you celebrate with us! Tag someone with an upcoming birthday to let them know about this special.

–

Encourage people to celebrate their birthdays at your restaurant. Offering a free dessert or appetizer is a great way to entice people to do so.

FEBRUARY 16TH

Gotta Love Memes

Do This: Find a funny food related meme to share with your audience. A good laugh can never hurt!

–

Who doesn't like a funny meme?

FEBRUARY 17TH

Random Act of Kindness Day

Caption: With today being #RandomActsOfKindnessDay, let's all share a random act of kindness that you've done for someone or someone has done for you!

–

Share a fun picture or quote and spread some positivity for Random Act of Kindness Day!

FEBRUARY 18TH

Happy Hour

Do This: Create a happy hour special. Share the details along with some photos of your refreshing drinks.

—

Having a happy hour is an excellent way to increase foot traffic and sales during the slower parts of the day.

FEBRUARY 19TH

Brunch Special

Do This: If you don't already have one, create a generous brunch special to drive morning traffic to your restaurant.

—

This is a great post to help spark people's taste buds and have them come by for a quick meal!

FEBRUARY 20TH

Featured Special of The Week

Do This: Every week showcase your featured special of the week alongside a mouth-watering photo of the dish.

–

Use this as an opportunity to showcase a popular dish that you are proud of and emphasize that it is only available this week to encourage your followers to come try it.

FEBRUARY 21ST

Highlighting a Review

Caption: This is what our amazing clients say about us! Thank you for your generous review [insert name]!

—

Reviews are arguably the most important part of a successful restaurant. Make sure to share and showcase those hard-earned stars across your social media platforms. Not only will this entice potential clients, but it will encourage previous clients to also leave kind remarks.

FEBRUARY 22ND

2-2-2 Special!

Do This: It's 2/22, which means we will be having our annual 2-2-2 special. Get 2 appetizers, 2 entrees and 2 desserts for just [insert price here]!

—

2-2-2 is a creative special that will get foodies flying in your door!

FEBRUARY 23RD

Local Trivia!

Caption: Let's see who knows [insert city name] best! [insert trivia question here].

—

Share a fun local trivia question with your followers!

FEBRUARY 24TH

Most Popular Plate

Caption: Tonight's most popular plate has by far been the [insert name of dish here]. [Add a more in-depth description here]!

—

Keep your followers informed on what's trending on your menu!

FEBRUARY 25TH

This or That

Do This: Showcase two popular entrees and have your followers choose which they would rather have!

–

'This or that' is an amazing conversation starter!

FEBRUARY 26TH

Sponsor a Local Event

Caption: We are proud sponsors of [event name]. Come join us for a fun, family friendly event.

–

Showcase your support for your community by sponsoring a local event!

FEBRUARY 28TH

Share a Customers Photo

Do This: Share a customer's photo that they posted on social media. Make sure to tag them and show your appreciation for them sharing their meal with the internet!

–

Word of mouth is the most powerful marketing tool. Sharing other customer photos will encourage others to share their photos online!

FEBRUARY 29TH

Food Photo of The Month

Caption: Introducing the February Food Photo of The Month! This amazing photo was taken by our lovely customer [insert name here] and features our signature [insert dish here].

—

The last day of the month is a great time to feature a beautiful photo taken by one of your customers!

MARCH 1ST

New Month New Food

Caption: Happy March! As we like to say.. New month, new food! Check out our recently added [insert name of dish here]

-

Use this as an opportunity to show off your newly added dishes on your menu.

MARCH 2ND

Featured Special of The Week

Do This: Every week showcase your featured special of the week alongside a mouth-watering photo of the dish.

—

Use this as an opportunity to showcase a popular dish that you are proud of and emphasize that it is only available this week to encourage your followers to come try it.

MARCH 3RD

Employee of The Month

Do This: Every month, recognize and profile one of your hard-working employees as "the employee of the month"

—

Although you may not initially think this is an impactful idea, customers love to get to know your staff. Showing your appreciation for your employees is also a great way to keep them motivated at work.

MARCH 4TH

Quote

Share This: "There is no sincerer love than the love of food."
– George Bernard Shaw

—

Share this foodie quote with your audience. Bonus points if you create a branded graphic with your logo on it rather than just sharing one off Google!

MARCH 5TH

Behind The Scenes!

Do This: Take a video showcasing a behind the scenes look at what it's like cooking up some delicious food at your restaurant!

-

High quality videos are a great way to keep your audience engaged along with allowing them to sed a different perspective compared to photos.

MARCH 6TH

Host an Event

Do this: Host a free event at your restaurant on a slow night to get extra foot traffic.

–

Consider hosting an art event, wine tasting or possibly even a book club at your restaurant! It's a great way to get locals familiar with your spot and make them more likely to come back for a meal.

MARCH 7TH

Sustainable

Do This: Showcase what your restaurant is doing to 'be green!' Being environmentally friendly and maintaining sustainable business practices is an important aspect to many diners!

—

Whether this means buying locally, educating your employees on sustainability, or managing your waste properly, little steps can make a big difference!

MARCH 8TH

International Women's Day

Caption: Happy International Women's Day to all the hard-working women in our community!

–

Today is a day to day celebrate the social, economic, cultural, and political achievements of women.

MARCH 9TH

Feature Regular Customers

Do This: Give a shoutout to one of your regular customers and have them share a quick story or what their favorite dish is!

—

Show appreciation to those who support you and your business day in and day out!

MARCH 10TH

Featured Special of The Week

Do This: Every week showcase your featured special of the week alongside a mouth-watering photo of the dish.

—

Use this as an opportunity to showcase a popular dish that you are proud of and emphasize that it is only available this week to encourage your followers to come try it.

MARCH 11TH

Signature Dish

Do This: Showcase a heavenly photo of one of your signature dishes!

—

In the restaurant business – the quality of your photos of social media goes a long way. Make sure to study up on some camera tips or hire a professional photographer to shoot your food.

MARCH 12TH

National Girl Scout® Day
Caption: It's National Girl Scout® Day! Did you grab a box of Girl Scout cookies® this year?

–

How can you not like Girl Scout cookies®!

MARCH 13TH

National Good Samaritan Day

Caption: Did you know it's National Good Samaritan Day? Today is a day to recognize the good deeds and unselfish actions of your neighbors. Make someone's day today!

-

It's a great day to make someone's day!

MARCH 14TH

Get to Know Us

Do This: Share your story of opening your restaurant. Think about these questions: who, what, where, when and why.

—

Building a strong support group around your establishment is about so much more than just food. Letting your customers know more about you and your story builds a more personal relationship.

MARCH 15TH

Food Prep

Do This: Share a photo or video of your staff food prepping for a big night!

–

People love the behind the scenes and seeing how fresh your food is! Use this as an opportunity to show the quality of what you serve to your customers.

MARCH 16TH

We Want to Know

Caption: We want to your favorite thing about us in one word! Is it the [insert popular dish] or the ambience or something else? Let us know in the comments below!

—

This is a great way to subtly ask for feedback. It's important to know what your customers like the most so you can make sure they get the best experience possible!

MARCH 17TH

Saint Patrick's Day

Caption: Happy Saint Patrick's Day from our family to yours!

–

Annual Saint Patrick's Day Post. If you are planning on having some specials — make sure to share them on your socials!

MARCH 18TH

Featured Special of The Week

Do This: Every week showcase your featured special of the week alongside a mouth-watering photo of the dish.

—

Use this as an opportunity to showcase a popular dish that you are proud of and emphasize that it is only available this week to encourage your followers to come try it.

MARCH 19TH

Merchandise for Sale

Do This: Consider selling some branded clothing for your hard-core fans!

—

There are tons of 'print on demand' online sites that also allow you to sell merchandise with no overhead cost!

MARCH 20TH

Value Through Video

Do This: Create a video of your staff welcoming customers into the store or explaining a special!

—

Videos are becoming a more and more prominent way to digest information through social media.

MARCH 21ST

FAQ

Do This: Answer some commonly asked questions about your food, hours, delivery etc.

—

If you are constantly getting calls or emails about a certain question, save yourself some time and answer it on social media!

MARCH 22ND

Competition

Do This: Organize a cook-off amongst restaurants near you for a certain type of food.

—

Whether it's just for fun or you incorporate a way to raise money for charity this is a great way to spread the word about your establishment, win or lose!

MARCH 23RD

Question

Caption: If you could only eat one thing off our menu for the rest of your life, what would it be?

—

This is a great post to get your followers to engage on your content. Who knows, they may end up craving their favorite food from your spot!

MARCH 24TH

New Menu Item

Do This: Spice it up and release a limited-edition menu item and showcase it with an irresistible photo!

—

In the restaurant business – the quality of your photos of social media goes a long way. Make sure to study up on some camera tips or hire a professional photographer to shoot your food.

MARCH 25TH

Quote

Share this: "Good Food Never Fail in Bringing People Together."
- Jatin and Kanika Khanna
-

Quotes are a great way to reach new followers. Share this quote along with a photo of your staff!

MARCH 26TH

Featured Special of The Week

Do This: Every week showcase your featured special of the week alongside a mouth-watering photo of the dish.

—

Use this as an opportunity to showcase a popular dish that you are proud of and emphasize that it is only available this week to encourage your followers to come try it.

MARCH 27TH

Local Trivia!

Caption: It's local trivia time! [insert trivia question here].

–

Share an interesting local trivia question and have your followers take a guess in the comments.

MARCH 28TH

Gotta Love Memes

Do This: Find a funny food related meme to share with your audience. A good laugh can never hurt!

–

Who doesn't like a funny meme?

MARCH 29TH

National Mom and Pop Business Owners Day

Caption: Happy National Mom and Pop Business Owners Day! Today I wanted to highlight one of my favorite small businesses. [Insert more details about them here]

-

Show your support local businesses.

MARCH 30TH

Appetizer or Dessert

Caption: If you had to choose, would you rather have [insert most popular appetizer] or [insert most popular dessert]?

—

I know choosing both would be the ideal option but showcase some of your most popular dishes with this fun competition. Not only will this show off your delicious food, but it will also encourage followers to get involved with this post.

MARCH 31ST

Food Photo of The Month

Caption: Introducing the March Food Photo of The Month! This amazing photo was taken by our lovely customer [insert name here] and features our signature [insert dish here].

-

The last day of the month is a great time to feature a beautiful photo taken by one of your customers!

APRIL 1ST

April Fools

Caption: Happy April Fool's day! What pranks are you pulling on your family today?

—

Who doesn't love a harmless April Fools prank?

APRIL 2ND

Employee of The Month

Do This: Every month, recognize and profile one of your hard-working employees as "the employee of the month"

–

Although you may not initially think this is an impactful idea, customers love to get to know your staff. Showing your appreciation for your employees is also a great way to keep them motivated at work.

APRIL 3RD

National Love Our Children Day

Do This: To celebrate National Love Our Children Day, offer a free meal for kids under the age of 12!

—

Show kids some extra love today with a fun discount. Make sure to add appropriate terms & conditions to this special.

APRIL 4TH

Featured Special of The Week

Do This: Every week showcase your featured special of the week alongside a mouth-watering photo of the dish.

—

Use this as an opportunity to showcase a popular dish that you are proud of and emphasize that it is only available this week to encourage your followers to come try it.

APRIL 5TH

Vegan Options

Do This: Share some of your vegan options with your audience.

—

Over the past few years, the number of vegans has risen dramatically. Share some dishes that are vegan friendly!

APRIL 6TH

Local Collaboration

Do This: Collaborate with a local business on a dish. Whether it be for their microgreens or fresh grown vegetables, it's always important to source your food locally when possible.

–

Showing your support for other local businesses while getting super fresh ingredients is a win, win!

APRIL 7TH

Signature Dish

Do This: Showcase a heavenly photo of one of your signature dishes!

—

In the restaurant business – the quality of your photos of social media goes a long way. Make sure to study up on some camera tips or hire a professional photographer to shoot your food.

APRIL 8TH

Share a Customers Photo

Do This: Share a customer's photo that they posted on social media. Make sure to tag them and show your appreciation for them sharing their meal with the internet!

–

Word of mouth is the most powerful marketing tool. Sharing other customer photos will encourage others to share their photos online!

APRIL 9TH

Highlighting a Review

Caption: Thank you for your kind words [Name of customer who shared the review]! Incredibly thankful for reviews like this. Definitely the most rewarding part of my job.

—

Reviews are arguably the most important part of a successful restaurant. Make sure to share and showcase those hard-earned stars across your social media platforms. Not only will this entice potential clients, but it will encourage previous clients to also leave kind remarks.

APRIL 10TH

Ask us Anything!

Caption: Have a question of any sorts? Whether it be allergy related or regarding catering, give us call today at 888-8888-8888!

–

Emphasize that you are here to help.

APRIL 11TH

Featured Special of The Week

Do This: Every week showcase your featured special of the week alongside a mouth-watering photo of the dish.

—

Use this as an opportunity to showcase a popular dish that you are proud of and emphasize that it is only available this week to encourage your followers to come try it.

APRIL 12TH

National Grilled Cheese Sandwich Day

Do This: Get creative and incorporate a limited-edition grilled cheese sandwich into your menu for National Grilled Cheese Sandwich Day.

—

Each year, National Grilled Cheese Sandwich Day is celebrated on April 12th.

APRIL 13TH

What's Hot

Do this: Share a professional photo of a dish that has been extremely popular lately!

–

Don't forget to brush up on your photography skills or hire a professional to make your social media as effective as possible!

APRIL 14TH

Take a Wild Guess Day

Caption: It's National Take a Wild Guess Day so it's only right to do some food trivia! [insert trivia question about your restaurant here].

-

If you are feeling generous give away a gift card to the winner.

APRIL 15TH

Tax Day

Caption: A friendly reminder that tax returns need to be post marked no later than today!

—

We all share the pain of taxes, but a friendly reminder never hurts.

APRIL 16TH

Food Blogger

Do this: Invite a local food blogger with a social media presence to eat at your restaurant for free!

—

In today's culture, one viral post from a well-known foodie can blow up your restaurant.

APRIL 17TH

This or That

Do This: Showcase two popular entrees and have your followers choose which they would rather have!

—

'This or that' is an amazing conversation starter!

APRIL 18TH

Foodie Checklist

Caption: Share a foodie must-try checklist with all your favorite dishes on your menu!

–

Post a branded graphic of a check list of must-try items at your restaurant!

APRIL 19TH

Create a Collage

Do This: Create a collage of 4 different entrees and have your followers choose which is their favorite!

–

This post is a great way to encourage followers to engage and comment on your content.

APRIL 20TH

Featured Special of The Week

Do This: Every week showcase your featured special of the week alongside a mouth-watering photo of the dish.

–

Use this as an opportunity to showcase a popular dish that you are proud of and emphasize that it is only available this week to encourage your followers to come try it.

APRIL 21ST

Restaurant Tour

Do This: Give a virtual video tour of your restaurant on social media.

—

Show off your restaurant and all the small details that often go unnoticed.

APRIL 22ND

Quote

Share This: "Hard work should be rewarded by good food."
- Ken Follett

—

Quotes are a great way to reach new followers. Funny, inspiring, and relatable sayings are bound to be shared amongst your followers, friends, and family.

APRIL 23RD

Cooking Lesson

Do This: Have your chef give a quick cooking lesson or tip via video!

—

This is a fun way to get your audience to get to know your chef and allow him/her to show off their talent!

APRIL 24ᵀᴴ

Run a Photo Contest

Do This: Run a photo contest of who can take the best photo of any entrée at your restaurant. Have them use a specific hashtag to enter so you can easily choose a winner!

—

Make the prize a dinner on you or a gift card to your restaurant. This is a fun way to get locals to spread the word about your restaurant on social media!

APRIL 25TH

Staff Bio

Do This: Share a short blurb about one of your employees alongside a photo of them!

—

Share their role at your restaurant along with anything they want to share about their life outside of work. Some examples are hobbies, family members, favorite food, etc.

APRIL 26TH

Highlighting a Review

Do This: Share a kind review from a customer of yours!

—

Reviews are arguably the most important part of a successful restaurant. Make sure to share and showcase those hard-earned stars across your social media platforms. Not only will this entice potential clients, but it will encourage previous clients to also leave kind remarks.

APRIL 27TH

National Tell a Story Day

Do This: Tell one of your favorite stories from your restaurant and share a photo along with it!

—

Every restaurant owner has some great stories, share one!

APRIL 28TH

Featured Special of The Week

Do This: Every week showcase your featured special of the week alongside a mouth-watering photo of the dish.

—

Use this as an opportunity to showcase a popular dish that you are proud of and emphasize that it is only available this week to encourage your followers to come try it.

APRIL 29TH

Upcoming Event

Do This: Promote an upcoming event that you are hosting at your restaurant! Whether it's a cooking class, open mic night or charity event, make sure to spread the word online!

—

If you're investing a lot of time into organizing events at your restaurant, you should be sharing them on all your social media platforms.

APRIL 30TH

Food Photo of The Month

Caption: Introducing the April Food Photo of The Month! This amazing photo was taken by our lovely customer [insert name here] and features our signature [insert dish here].

-

The last day of the month is a great time to feature a beautiful photo taken by one of your customers!

MAY 1ST

Employee of The Month

Do This: Every month, recognize and profile one of your hard-working employees as "the employee of the month"

–

Although you may not initially think this is an impactful idea, customers love to get to know your staff. Showing your appreciation for your employees is also a great way to keep them motivated at work.

MAY 2ND

Gluten-Free Menu Options

Do This: Share some gluten-free options with your following!

-

According to a study done by Statistica, " eight percent of people followed a wheat-free or gluten-free diet as of 2016."

MAY 3RD

Gotta Love Memes

Do This: Find a funny food related meme to share with your audience. A good laugh can never hurt!

–

Who doesn't like a funny meme?

MAY 4TH

Creative Food Photos

Do This: Take some creative photos of some of your latest dishes and share them online with your audience.

–

Food Photography Tip: Move around to find the best light source. Don't feel confined to taking photos in your kitchen

MAY 5TH

Charity Event

Caption: Partner with a charity and donate a portion of your proceeds.

—

As a small business, getting involved in local charities is an excellent way to raise money for a good deed along with establishing your businesses credibility around town.

MAY 6TH

Featured Special of The Week

Do This: Every week showcase your featured special of the week alongside a mouth-watering photo of the dish.

–

Use this as an opportunity to showcase a popular dish that you are proud of and emphasize that it is only available this week to encourage your followers to come try it.

MAY 7TH

Now Taking Bookings for Mother's Day

Do this: Create a post letting your audience know that you are now taking lunch and dinner reservations for Mother's Day!

–

Mother's Day reservations usually book up fast so make sure to let your loyal social media followers get first dibs!

MAY 8TH

Share a Customers Photo

Do This: Share a customer's photo that they posted on social media. Make sure to tag them and show your appreciation for them sharing their meal with the internet!

—

Word of mouth is the most powerful marketing tool. Sharing other customer photos will encourage others to share their photos online!

MAY 9TH

Meet The Chefs

Do This: Create a post introducing your chef/s and give a little background on each of them.

—

People love to meet and get to know the people behind all your delicious food.

MAY 10TH

Dinner is Just a Phone Call Away!

Do This: Encourage people to call in for take-out! Make sure to include your phone number along with your website If they can order online.

-

Did you know that 60% of U.S. consumers order delivery or takeout once a week? (Statistic via: Upserve.com)

MAY 11TH

2 For...

Do This: Create a special that allows 2 people to eat for an affordable price! Use social media as a platform to get the word out.

—

Specials are a great way to attract new customers. Who knows maybe they will turn in to regulars!

MAY 12TH

Today Only

Do This: Offer a special deal or meal of some sort that is only available today.

—

This is a great incentive to get people into your restaurant to try something new!

MAY 13TH

Highlighting a Review

Caption: Thank you for your kind words [Name of customer who shared the review]! Thank you for choosing us time and time again.

—

Reviews are arguably the most important part of a successful restaurant. Make sure to share and showcase those hard-earned stars across your social media platforms. Not only will this entice potential clients, but it will encourage previous clients to also leave kind remarks.

MAY 14TH

Featured Special of The Week

Do This: Every week showcase your featured special of the week alongside a mouth-watering photo of the dish.

–

Use this as an opportunity to showcase a popular dish that you are proud of and emphasize that it is only available this week to encourage your followers to come try it.

MAY 15TH

National Chocolate Chip Day

Do This: Get creative and establish a limited-edition chocolate chip dessert.

–

National Chocolate Chip Day is celebrated on May 15th of every year. Make today special with a fun dessert made with chocolate chips.

MAY 16TH

A Drink on the House

Do this: Offer a refreshing drink on the house with any entrée purchase to drive more foot traffic!

–

This is an inexpensive way to attract more diners to come have a meal at your restaurant.

MAY 17TH

QR Code

Do This: Share a post with a QR code that links to your menu saying "Hungry? Come try our new [insert special] tonight!"

—

QR codes are an easy way to give people instant access to your menu on social media! (Also make sure to mention that the link in your bio directs to your site in case they aren't familiar with QR codes)

MAY 18TH

Quote

Share This: "Good food, good people, good times!"

–

Quotes are a great way to reach new followers. Funny, inspiring, and relatable sayings are bound to be shared amongst your followers, friends, and family.

MAY 19TH

This or That

Do This: Showcase two popular entrees and have your followers choose which they would rather have!

–

'This or that' is an amazing conversation starter!

MAY 20TH

Chef's Choice

Do This: Share a photo and description of one of your chef's favorite menu items!

–

Who wouldn't trust a chef when it comes to choosing their entrée?

MAY 21ST

Would You Rather?

Caption: Would you rather have our [insert entrée name here] or our [insert entrée name here]!

—

'Would you rather' posts are a great way to get your audience engaged by having them comment which dish they would prefer.

MAY 22ND

Featured Special of The Week

Do This: Every week showcase your featured special of the week alongside a mouth-watering photo of the dish.

—

Use this as an opportunity to showcase a popular dish that you are proud of and emphasize that it is only available this week to encourage your followers to come try it.

MAY 23RD

Cup of Coffee

Do This: Share a photo of a piping hot cup of coffee!

—

If your restaurant doesn't serve coffee share a photo of a different type of drink!

MAY 24TH

Take Out Special

Do This: Offer an exclusive take out special for those who follow you on social media!

–

Use this as an opportunity to showcase some of the perks of following you on social media!

MAY 25TH

National Wine Day

Do This: It's National Wine Day! If you serve wine share a photo of a glass of wine and say "Today, wine enthusiasts pour a glass of their favorite wine to celebrate National Wine Day!"

–

If you don't serve wine, consider sharing a photo of a beautifully plated entrée.

MAY 26TH

Get Your Followers Involved

Do This: Create a post that will get your followers involved and make them feel like a part of your restaurant. Consider launching a new menu item and letting followers comment creative names for the item!

-

Consider rewarding the follower with a free meal if their proposed name is chosen to be on the menu!

MAY 27TH

Lunch Special

Do This: Create a lunch special! Offering promotions is a great way for you to attract a new customer who have been thinking about giving your spot a try.

—

Offer a lunch special to intrigue your followers to come in for a delicious and affordable meal!

MAY 28TH

Hamburger Day

Do This: It's National Hamburger Day! Come up with a creative limited-edition burger to serve today!

—

If you don't serve burgers, it's also National Brisket Day — consider trying to incorporate either of these into your menu if possible!

MAY 29TH

Featured Special of The Week

Do This: Every week showcase your featured special of the week alongside a mouth-watering photo of the dish.

—

Use this as an opportunity to showcase a popular dish that you are proud of and emphasize that it is only available this week to encourage your followers to come try it.

MAY 30TH

Highlighting a Review

Caption: Thank you for your 5-star review [Name of customer who shared the review]!

—

Reviews are arguably the most important part of a successful restaurant. Make sure to share and showcase those hard-earned stars across your social media platforms. Not only will this entice potential clients, but it will encourage previous clients to also leave kind remarks.

MAY 31ST

Food Photo of The Month

Caption: Introducing the May Food Photo of The Month! This amazing photo was taken by our lovely customer [insert name here] and features our signature [insert dish here].

-

The last day of the month is a great time to feature a beautiful photo taken by one of your customers!

JUNE 1ST

Employee of The Month

Do This: Every month, recognize and profile one of your hard-working employees as "the employee of the month"

–

Although you may not initially think this is an impactful idea, customers love to get to know your staff. Showing your appreciation for your employees is also a great way to keep them motivated at work.

JUNE 2ND

Share a Recipe

Do This: Share a recipe of one of your dishes with your audience!

—

Contrary to popular belief, sharing recipes for some of your dishes does not diminish your brand value. Recipes deepen the bond between your food and your clientele and prove your expertise even more.

JUNE 3RD

Gotta Love Memes

Do This: Find a funny food related meme to share with your audience. A good laugh can never hurt!

–

Who doesn't like a funny meme?

JUNE 4TH

National Cheese Day

Do This: It's National Cheese Day! Come up with a creative limited-edition dish featuring a fancy cheese to serve today!

–

If National Cheese Day is a no-go for you, it's also National Donut Day!

JUNE 5TH

Things To Do This Weekend

Caption: Share a list of local events or something fun to do this weekend!

–

Use this post to showcase your sense of community.

JUNE 6TH

Featured Special of The Week

Do This: Every week showcase your featured special of the week alongside a mouth-watering photo of the dish.

—

Use this as an opportunity to showcase a popular dish that you are proud of and emphasize that it is only available this week to encourage your followers to come try it.

JUNE 7TH

Advertise an Appetizer

Caption: Let's be real, our appetizers are way underrated! Have you tried our [title of your dish]?

—

Appetizers never get enough social buzz! Use this as an opportunity to showcase your most popular appetizer!

JUNE 8TH

Ask a Question

Do This: Ask your audience a question. Ex: what kind of specials do you want to see from us this month?

—

Getting your audience involved will make them feel like family. It's so important to listen to the people that are supporting you.

JUNE 9TH

Quote

Share a quote: "Love at first bite" – our clients

—

Quotes are a great way to reach new followers. Funny, inspiring, and relatable sayings are bound to be shared amongst your followers, friends, and family.

JUNE 10TH

National Iced Tea Day

Caption: It's National Iced Tea Day! Have you tried our [insert ice tea name here].

—

Celebrated every year on June 10th, National Iced Tea Day toast's to one of summer's favorite drinks.

JUNE 11TH

Famous Person

Do This: Have you ever had a famous person or local celebrity stop by for a meal? If so – share their photo on social media!

-

This will help build your sense of credibility online knowing celebrities have dined with you!

JUNE 12TH

What's Trending

Do This: Share a photo of a trending special that everyone has been loving!

−

If the photo looks delicious – people will come in to try it!

JUNE 13TH

This or That

Do This: Showcase two popular entrees and have your followers choose which they would rather have!

–

'This or that' is an amazing conversation starter!

JUNE 14TH

Featured Special of The Week

Do This: Every week showcase your featured special of the week alongside a mouth-watering photo of the dish.

—

Use this as an opportunity to showcase a popular dish that you are proud of and emphasize that it is only available this week to encourage your followers to come try it.

JUNE 15TH

Catering

Do This: Let your followers know that you offer catering services for parties!

—

Not only is catering a great way to sell bulk food but also a great way to get the message out about your restaurant. Often, guests at the party will ask the host where they catered from, and word will spread quickly!

JUNE 16TH

Staff Bio

Do This: Share a short blurb about one of your employees alongside a photo of them!

—

Share their role at your restaurant along with anything they want to share about their life outside of work. Some examples are hobbies, family members, favorite food, etc.

JUNE 17TH

Signature Dish

Do This: Showcase a heavenly photo of one of your signature dishes!

—

In the restaurant business – the quality of your photos of social media goes a long way. Make sure to study up on some camera tips or hire a professional photographer to shoot your food.

JUNE 18TH

Tasting Event

Do This: Host a food/wine tasting event at your restaurant where people can come in for a set price and try unlimited food in small portions.

—

This is a great way to attract new customers to come in and try a bunch of different dishes for an affordable price!

JUNE 19TH

National Martini Day

Do This: If you offer Martini's do something special for National Martini Day!

-

If you don't serve alcohol, consider serving a limited-edition non-alcoholic martini (dry martini).

JUNE 20TH

Bottomless Brunch

Do This: Offer a bottomless brunch special where customers can get unlimited brunch food for a fixed rate.

—

Don't get this confused with the bottomless brunch that refers to drinks. According to Bustle, there are 23 states that prohibit "bottomless brunches" and any other unlimited drink deal for a set cost and time.

JUNE 21ᵀᴴ

National Selfie Day

Do This: Take a selfie with your hardworking team and show your appreciation for who you get to work with on a daily basis.

-

Fun fact: The first time National Selfie Day was celebrated was on June 21, 2014.

JUNE 22ND

Featured Special of The Week

Do This: Every week showcase your featured special of the week alongside a mouth-watering photo of the dish.

—

Use this as an opportunity to showcase a popular dish that you are proud of and emphasize that it is only available this week to encourage your followers to come try it.

JUNE 23RD

Highlighting a Review

Caption: Thank your 5-star review [Name of customer who shared the review]! We appreciate all of you that take the time to leave kind reviews!

—

Reviews are arguably the most important part of a successful restaurant. Make sure to share and showcase those hard-earned stars across your social media platforms. Not only will this entice potential clients, but it will encourage previous clients to also leave kind remarks.

JUNE 24TH

Signature Sauce

Do This: Have you noticed signature sauces are SO popular? If you don't already have one, create a signature sauce and share a heavenly photo of it with your audience.

—

This might sound crazy but think of all the people that are obsessed with Chick-fil-A® sauce. Create something unique and delicious and who knows, your sauce could go viral and be in stores in a matter of months!

JUNE 25TH

Host a Competition

Do This: Host a fun competition where everyone who eats at your restaurant for the next week is entered into a raffle to win something!

—

Whether you give away tickets to a sought-after local event or a gift card to your restaurant, this is a great way to entice people to stop by for a meal.

JUNE 26TH

Show Your Restaurant!

Do This: Take a photo of your restaurant with all the tables set and say, "We are ready for a busy night at [insert restaurant name here]."

—

Show off your restaurant's atmosphere with a photo of all the tables set and ready for guests!

JUNE 27TH

Share an Interesting Fact
Example: Did you know we source all our fresh greens from a local farm just 20 minutes away from our restaurant?

-

There are tons of benefits to using locally produced food in your restaurant. By doing this you are supporting your community's economy.

JUNE 28TH

Value Through Video

Do This: Show your chefs in action! Take a video of your chef's prepping a meal in the kitchen.

—

Videos are becoming a more and more prominent and effective way to digest information through social media.

JUNE 29TH

Social Media Day

Do This: Share a few of your favorite foodie pages to follow on social media!

—

There are so many amazing food niche pages to follow across various social media platforms!

JUNE 30TH

Food Photo of The Month

Caption: Introducing the June Food Photo of The Month! This amazing photo was taken by our lovely customer [insert name here] and features our signature [insert dish here].

-

The last day of the month is a great time to feature a beautiful photo taken by one of your customers!

JULY 1ST

Employee of The Month

Do This: Every month, recognize and profile one of your hard-working employees as "the employee of the month"

−

Although you may not initially think this is an impactful idea, customers love to get to know your staff. Showing your appreciation for your employees is also a great way to keep them motivated at work.

JULY 2ND

Featured Special of The Week

Do This: Every week showcase your featured special of the week alongside a mouth-watering photo of the dish.

—

Use this as an opportunity to showcase a popular dish that you are proud of and emphasize that it is only available this week to encourage your followers to come try it.

JULY 3RD

Showcase Your Plating

Do This: Take a photo of a dish beautifully plated and share it on all your socials!

–

Knocking the presentation of a dish out of the park adds tremendous value to the experience of dining out.

JULY 4TH

4th of July!

Do This: Wish everyone a Happy 4th of July along with a patriotic graphic

—

Make sure this post is red, white, and blue!

JULY 5TH

Share a Customers Photo

Do This: Share a customer's photo that they posted on social media. Make sure to tag them and show your appreciation for them sharing their meal with the internet!

–

Word of mouth is the most powerful marketing tool. Sharing other customer photos will encourage others to share their photos online!

JULY 6TH

National Fried Chicken Day

Do This: It's National Fried Chicken Day! Come up with a crispy limited-edition chicken sandwich featuring your signature sauce!

–

If a chicken sandwich doesn't fit in on your menu, consider just sharing one of your chicken dishes.

JULY 7TH

Gotta Love Memes

Do This: Find a funny food related meme to share with your audience. A good laugh can never hurt!

–

Who doesn't like a funny meme?

JULY 8TH

Would You Rather

Ask This: Are you more of a dine in person or would you rather take out?

–

Get the comment section buzzing with a fun interactive question!

JULY 9TH

Live Stream

Do This: Do a quick live stream event with one of your chef's showing how to make a certain dish!

—

Live streams are becoming more and more popular on social media platforms like as Instagram and Facebook.

JULY 10TH

Featured Special of The Week

Do This: Every week showcase your featured special of the week alongside a mouth-watering photo of the dish.

—

Use this as an opportunity to showcase a popular dish that you are proud of and emphasize that it is only available this week to encourage your followers to come try it.

JULY 11TH

Partner With a Local Business

Do This: Partner with a local business! Example: Collaborate with a local spice shop and incorporate one of their unique spices on your dishes.

—

This is a great way to show your love for your community and support for local businesses. If people love the dish – consider having a stock of the spices in your store for customers to purchase!

JULY 12TH

Food Facts

Do This: Share an interesting food fact related to your restaurant.

—

Example (if you serve a dish with corn): Did you know that corn always has an even number of rows on each ear?

JULY 13TH

$20 Special

Do This: Create a $20 special and share it through a branded graphic on social media!

–

Getting people to try your food is the first step to becoming a successful restaurant. Once you get people in the door and realize how good your food is, they will keep coming back.

JULY 14TH

Highlighting a Review

Caption: Thank your kind review [Name of customer who shared the review]! We are so glad we were able to satisfy your taste buds!

—

Reviews are arguably the most important part of a successful restaurant. Make sure to share and showcase those hard-earned stars across your social media platforms. Not only will this entice potential clients, but it will encourage previous clients to also leave kind remarks.

JULY 15TH

Get to Know Your Customers Day

Caption: It's Get to Know Your Customers Day! Stop by to say hello and grab a free cup of coffee on us!

–

Get to Know Your Customers Day is all about going the extra mile to get to know the people who support you!

JULY 16TH

National Personal Chef's Day

Do This: Although your chef isn't technically a personal chef, share a photo and message from your chef thanking your followers for all their support!

—

Each year, National Personal Chef Day is celebrated on July 16th to recognize the hard work of chefs across the United States.

JULY 17TH

Feature Regular Customers

Do This: Give a shoutout to one of your regular customers and have them share a quick story or what their favorite dish is!

—

Show appreciation to those who support you and your business day in and day out!

JULY 18TH

National Ice Cream Month

Do this: Share an ice cream infused dessert for National Ice Cream Month!

—

July is National Ice Cream Month along with National Ice Cream Day being celebrated on the third Sunday in July, in the United States.

JULY 19TH

Featured Special of The Week

Do This: Every week showcase your featured special of the week alongside a mouth-watering photo of the dish.

-

Use this as an opportunity to showcase a popular dish that you are proud of and emphasize that it is only available this week to encourage your followers to come try it.

JULY 20TH

Milestone

Do this: Have you hit a milestone recently? Whether that be social media followers, years open or something else, make sure to share that milestone online and thank your customers for everything they do!

—

It's so important to show appreciation toward your customers. Doing so reflects a positively on your company and shows that you value those who support you.

JULY 21ST

What's Trending

Do This: Share a photo of a trending special that everyone has been loving!

–

If the photo looks delicious – people will come in to try it!

JULY 22ND

National Refreshment Day

Do This: Share one of your most popular refreshments for #NationalRefreshmentDay.

—

Make sure to double check this date as National Refreshment Day changes every year. It is celebrated annually on the fourth Thursday of July!

JULY 23ʳᴰ

10% Off Take Out

Do This: Offer 10% off take-out orders today only!

-

Since the pandemic, take out numbers have skyrocketed. Encourage people to order and pick up from your spot with this offer!

JULY 24TH

Share Community Involvement

Do This: Get involved with your community at a local event or street fair! Share some photos of the event.

—

As a small business owner – getting involved with your local community is key to building a strong following around your restaurant.

JULY 25TH

National Wine and Cheese Day

Caption: It's National Wine and Cheese Day! What is your favorite wine and cheese combination?

—

It's National Wine and Cheese Day, and it's a day that's celebrated on July 25th every year. Share a photo of wine and cheese to celebrate. If this doesn't seem like a fit for your restaurant also consider celebrating National Hot Fudge Sundae Day which is today as well!

JULY 26TH

Featured In!

Do this: Share some of your best food photos with small to medium sized food niche pages to score a feature. Once you are featured – repost the image across your platforms!

-

Being featured in food pages with a decent following is a great credibility booster along with sending some traffic towards your restaurant!

JULY 27TH

Featured Special of The Week

Do This: Every week showcase your featured special of the week alongside a mouth-watering photo of the dish.

—

Use this as an opportunity to showcase a popular dish that you are proud of and emphasize that it is only available this week to encourage your followers to come try it.

JULY 28TH

Showcase Your Plating

Do This: Take a photo of a dish beautifully plated and share it on all your socials!

—

Knocking the presentation of a dish out of the park adds tremendous value to the experience of dining out.

JULY 29TH

Let's Talk

Caption: Ask us anything about our menu! Drop a line below and let's get your questions answered.

—

Share a photo of your menu and allow your followers to use the comment section as a forum to get their questions answered.

JULY 30TH

Did you know...
Do This: Share a photo of a certain dish along with a fun fact about it!

–

Example: Did you know that our Parmesan cheese we use in our Parmigiano Reggiano Mac and Cheese comes straight from Italy?

JULY 31ST

Food Photo of The Month

Caption: Introducing the July Food Photo of The Month! This amazing photo was taken by our lovely customer [insert name here] and features our signature [insert dish here].

-

The last day of the month is a great time to feature a beautiful photo taken by one of your customers!

AUGUST 1ST

New Month New Food

Caption: Happy August! As we like to say.. New month, new food! Check out our recently added [insert name of dish here]

–

Use this as an opportunity to show off your newly added dishes on your menu.

AUGUST 2ND

Share a Recipe

Do This: Share a recipe of one of your dishes with your audience!

—

Contrary to popular belief, sharing recipes for some of your dishes does not diminish your brand value. Recipes deepen the bond between your food and your clientele and prove your expertise even more.

AUGUST 3ʳᵈ

Staff Picks!

Do This: Share some of your staff's favorite dishes. Post a photo of them and their favorite menu-item along with a short description of why it's their go-to.

—

Customers always ask their waiters for recommendations, and this is a fun way to do something similar online!

AUGUST 4TH

Featured Special of The Week

Do This: Every week showcase your featured special of the week alongside a mouth-watering photo of the dish.

–

Use this as an opportunity to showcase a popular dish that you are proud of and emphasize that it is only available this week to encourage your followers to come try it.

AUGUST 5TH

Cooking Lesson

Do This: Have your chef give a quick cooking lesson or tip via video!

—

This is a fun way to get your audience to get to know your chef and allow him/her to show off their talent!

AUGUST 6TH

Quote

Share this: "One cannot think well, love well, sleep well, if one has not dined well."
- Virginia Woolf
-

Quotes are a great way to reach new followers. Funny, inspiring, and relatable sayings are bound to be shared amongst your followers, friends, and family.

AUGUST 7TH

This or That

Do This: Showcase two popular entrees and have your followers choose which they would rather have!

–

'This or that' is an amazing conversation starter!

AUGUST 8TH

Staff Takeover

Do This: Assign a trusted staff member to take over your social media for the day and have them create videos walking your followers through a day in the life working at your restaurant.

—

Believe it or not, this is a super popular trend as people love to get a behind the scenes look at the restaurant business!

AUGUST 9TH

National Book Lovers Day

Do this: Share some of your favorite cookbooks and encourage your audience to do the same!

–

National Book Lovers Day is celebrated on August 9th every year.

AUGUST 10TH

Free Food
Do This: Offer 5 followers to try one of your new dishes for free!

–

In return for the free meal, they must post a photo on social media and/or review you on Google or Yelp!

AUGUST 11TH

Gift Cards

Caption: Give more, love more! Did you know we offer gift cards? Stop by during business hours or give us a call at 888-888-8888 to grab yours.

-

Let your followers know that you have gift certificates available for purchase!

AUGUST 12TH

Featured Special of The Week

Do This: Every week showcase your featured special of the week alongside a mouth-watering photo of the dish.

—

Use this as an opportunity to showcase a popular dish that you are proud of and emphasize that it is only available this week to encourage your followers to come try it.

AUGUST 13TH

National Filet Mignon Day

Do This: If your establishment serves Filet Mignon, share a mouth-watering photo of the dish!

—

National Filet Mignon Day is celebrated annually on August 13th.

AUGUST 14TH

Featured in the News?

Do This: If your establishment has recently been featured in the news, share the article with your followers!

–

Press is a great way to establish credibility as a business owner. If you have been featured in multiple different news sites, consider adding: As seen in: [insert news sites here] to your bio.

AUGUST 15TH

Featured Drink

Caption: We've got some delicious, featured drinks going this month. Check out our [describe drink here].

-

Whether it's a wine, coffee or an over-the-top milkshake, share a drink that everyone has been loving!

AUGUST 16TH

National Tell a Joke Day
Share this: Share a food-related joke or meme that you found online!

–

There are so many hilarious food memes on social media!

AUGUST 17TH

Ask a Question

Do this: Ask whether your followers prefer [insert dish] over [insert dish].

—

Getting your customers involved is a huge part about curating a strong relationship with your followers online!

AUGUST 18TH

Cooking Tips

Do This: Have your chef share some valuable cooking tips through a video.

—

Videos are becoming a more and more prominent way to digest information through social media.

AUGUST 19TH

Restaurant History

Caption: Share some history fun facts about your restaurant that most of your followers don't know!

—

Believe it or not, people love to know the history behind a restaurant.

AUGUST 20TH

Featured Special of The Week

Do This: Every week showcase your featured special of the week alongside a mouth-watering photo of the dish.

—

Use this as an opportunity to showcase a popular dish that you are proud of and emphasize that it is only available this week to encourage your followers to come try it.

AUGUST 21ST

National Senior Citizens Day

Do This: Offer a senior citizen discount for National Senior Citizens Day!

—

National Senior Citizens Day is celebrated annually on August 21st.

AUGUST 22ND

Sponsor a Local Event

Do This: Get your name out there by sponsoring a local event. Share your banner or ad on social media to show your support for your community

—

Getting your name out there locally is key to a successful small business. When community members notice your local support, they will be sure to support your restaurant as well1

AUGUST 23RD

Family Takeout Meal

Do This: Create and promote a family sized take out bundle!

–

Having a family sized bundle makes ordering convenient for your customers.

AUGUST 24TH

TV Shows

Caption: What is everyone's favorite food reality show? I recently just watched [Insert show here] and absolutely loved it!

-

Who doesn't love a little foodie TV action!

AUGUST 25TH

Food Blogger

Do this: Invite a local food blogger with a social media presence to eat at your restaurant for free!

–

In today's culture, one viral post from a well-known foodie can blow up your restaurant.

AUGUST 26TH

Showcase Some Behind the Scenes Content

Do This: Share a photo or a video showcasing the behind the scenes of your restaurant.

–

Whether this is showing your employees getting ready for a busy night or your chef preparing the food, social media loves to see the behind the scenes.

AUGUST 25TH

Live Music

Do This: Host an open mic night or have live music at your restaurant!

—

As silly as this may sound, high quality restaurant music can attract more customers and encourage them to spend more on a meal!

AUGUST 26TH

National Dog Day

Do This: Share a photo of your dog in front of your restaurant (if you have one) with the hashtag #NationalDogDay.

—

Who doesn't love dogs!

AUGUST 27TH

National Just Because Day

Do This: Host a fun social media give away just because! Ideas: a gift card to your restaurant, a free dessert, etc.

–

Have people enter by requiring them to follow you and tagging three friends in the comments. This will help boost your footprint on social media!

AUGUST 28TH

Featured Special of The Week

Do This: Every week showcase your featured special of the week alongside a mouth-watering photo of the dish.

–

Use this as an opportunity to showcase a popular dish that you are proud of and emphasize that it is only available this week to encourage your followers to come try it.

AUGUST 29TH

Highlighting a Review

Caption: Thank you [name of client] for your kind review! We can't wait to see you back soon.

—

Reviews are arguably the most important part of a successful restaurant. Make sure to share and showcase those hard-earned stars across your social media platforms. Not only will this entice potential clients, but it will encourage previous clients to also leave kind remarks.

AUGUST 30TH

Local Collaboration

Do This: Collaborate with a local business on social media. Example: Collaborate with an ice cream store across the street.

–

Take a photo of your dish alongside a sundae from their ice cream shop and say "[insert your restaurants name] and [insert their restaurants name] is the perfect combo on a hot summer night." If both of you post it and tag each other it's a win, win for everyone!

AUGUST 31ST

Food Photo of The Month

Caption: Introducing the August Food Photo of The Month! This amazing photo was taken by our lovely customer [insert name here] and features our signature [insert dish here].

—

The last day of the month is a great time to feature a beautiful photo taken by one of your customers!

SEPTEMBER 1ST

New Month New Food

Caption: Happy September! As we like to say.. New month, new food! Check out our recently added [insert name of dish here]

-

Use this as an opportunity to show off your newly added dishes on your menu.

SEPTEMBER 2ND

Signature Dish

Do This: Showcase a heavenly photo of one of your signature dishes!

—

In the restaurant business – the quality of your photos of social media goes a long way. Make sure to study up on some camera tips or hire a professional photographer to shoot your food.

SEPTEMBER 3ᴿᴰ

Staff Bio

Do This: Share a short blurb about one of your employees alongside a photo of them!

—

Share their role at your restaurant along with anything they want to share about their life outside of work. Some examples are hobbies, family members, favorite food, etc.

SEPTEMBER 4TH

Featured Special of The Week

Do This: Every week showcase your featured special of the week alongside a mouth-watering photo of the dish.

—

Use this as an opportunity to showcase a popular dish that you are proud of and emphasize that it is only available this week to encourage your followers to come try it.

SEPTEMBER 4TH

Gotta Love Memes

Do This: Find a funny food related meme to share with your audience. A good laugh can never hurt!

–

Who doesn't like a funny meme?

SEPTEMBER 5TH

Cheese Pizza Day

Do This: It's #CheesePizzaDay, share a photo of a pizza at your restaurant if you sell pizza, or if not, feature your favorite pizza place in town!

-

Who doesn't love a piping hot slice of cheese pizza?

SEPTEMBER 6TH

Give Notice for an Upcoming Promotion

Do This: Keep your followers in the loop on any upcoming promotions you may be having.

-

Use social media to get people excited and book a reservation to your restaurant!

SEPTEMBER 7TH

Quote

Share this: "Food is our common ground, a universal experience." - James Beard

—

Quotes are a great way to reach new followers. Funny, inspiring, and relatable sayings are bound to be shared amongst your followers, friends, and family.

SEPTEMBER 8TH

Local Author Book Signing
Do This: Reach out to a local author and see if they'd be interested in coming by and doing a book signing in the front part of your restaurant!

-

Have your town put this as an event on the town website and you will drive lots of traffic to your restaurant!

SEPTEMBER 9TH

Appetizer or Dessert

Caption: If you had to choose, would you rather have [insert most popular appetizer] or [insert most popular dessert]?

–

I know choosing both would be the ideal option but showcase some of your most popular dishes with this fun competition. Not only will this show off your delicious food, but it will also encourage followers to engage on the post.

SEPTEMBER 10TH

World Suicide Prevention Day
Caption: Today is World Suicide Prevention Day. Please know you matter. If you are ever feeling down or just simply need someone to talk to please do not hesitate to reach out.

—

Use your platform to raise awareness for suicide prevention.

SEPTEMBER 11TH

Upcoming Events

Do This: Create a post sharing upcoming events in your town.

—

Most towns have a town calendar that you can pull events from.

SEPTEMBER 12TH

National Day of Encouragement

Do This: Take a video of a staff member spreading some type of encouragement on social media. Whether it's lifting someone up when their down or simply motivating someone, today is an excellent day to do that.

—

National Day Of Encouragement is a holiday that falls on September 12th annually

SEPTEMBER 13TH

Featured Special of The Week

Do This: Every week showcase your featured special of the week alongside a mouth-watering photo of the dish.

—

Use this as an opportunity to showcase a popular dish that you are proud of and emphasize that it is only available this week to encourage your followers to come try it.

SEPTEMBER 14TH

Delivery Services

Do this: Share a post that lets your followers know all the delivery services where you can order from.

—

Is your restaurant on Door Dash®, Uber Eats® and a million other delivery services? Make sure to let your followers know where they can find you!

SEPTEMBER 15TH

Charity Event

Caption: Partner with a charity and donate a portion of your proceeds.

—

As a small business getting involved in local charities is an excellent way to raise money for a good deed along with establishing your businesses credibility around town.

SEPTEMBER 16TH

National Double Cheeseburger Day

Do this: Post a photo of one of your cheeseburgers (if you serve them) or your favorite local burger joint!

-

Today is a holiday that celebrates one of the most iconic American food items: burgers.

SEPTEMBER 17TH

This Weeks Favorites

Do This: Showcase some of the most popular dishes on your menu this week!

–

Share some photos along with a short description of each dish!

SEPTEMBER 18TH

What Goes Together

Do This: Share a photo of a drink and entrée that go together perfectly.

–

Make sure to let people know what they are called in the caption so they can reference this post when they go to order!

SEPTEMBER 19TH

FAQ

Do This: Post a commonly asked question and answer to a query you get often.

—

FAQ's are a great way to answer questions on a larger scale.

SEPTEMBER 20TH

Did you know...

Do This: Share a fun fact about your food or your restaurant that most of your followers wouldn't know!

–

Believe it or not, people love to know the story behind a restaurant.

SEPTEMBER 21ᵀᴴ

National New York Day
Do This: Share a New York inspired dish for #NationalNewYorkDay

–

Who doesn't love the big city?

SEPTEMBER 22ND

Value Through Video
Do This: Create a video of you inside your kitchen showcasing one of your cooks making a popular dish or plating food!

-

Videos are becoming a more and more prominent and accessible way to digest information through social media.

SEPTEMBER 23ᴿᴰ

Featured Special of The Week

Do This: Every week showcase your featured special of the week alongside a mouth-watering photo of the dish.

-

Use this as an opportunity to showcase a popular dish that you are proud of and emphasize that it is only available this week to encourage your followers to come try it.

SEPTEMBER 24ᵀᴴ

How Are We Doing?

Caption: We'd love to know how your experience was with us! Feel free to drop us a direct message or review us letting us know how everything was.

—

Encourage your followers to write a review or send you a direct message with any queries they may have about their experience with you!

SEPTEMBER 25TH

Food Prep

Do This: Share a photo or video of food prepping for a big night!

—

People love the behind the scenes and seeing how fresh your food is! Use this as an opportunity to show the quality of what you serve to your customers.

SEPTEMBER 26TH

Allergies?

Do This: Lots of people have allergies and certain dietary needs. Mention some of your dishes that are dairy free, nut free or gluten free.

–

Eating out with certain dietary needs can be extremely difficult. Creating this informative post will make it much easier!

SEPTEMBER 27TH

Showcase a Dessert

Do This: Post a photo of one of your most popular dessert's.

–

Simply glancing at a photo of a mouth-watering dessert is enough to get many people to book a reservation! (Including myself)

SEPTEMBER 28TH

National Good Neighbor Day
Do This: Share something you love about your neighbors and do something nice for them. Good, thoughtful neighbors make everything 10x easier.

–

This could be your businesses neighbors or your neighbors at home!

SEPTEMBER 29TH

National Coffee Day

Do This: Show off a photo of a cup of coffee (if you serve it) or your favorite local coffee shop and encourage others to do the same.

-

If you are feeling generous maybe even use this as an opportunity to do a giveaway to drive more followers to your page!

SEPTEMBER 30TH

Reminder

Caption: You don't need to spend money to support a local business. Write a review, follow them on social media or refer them when appropriate.

-

It's important to support local businesses within your community! Supporting them doesn't always have to mean spending money.

SEPTEMBER 31ᵀᴴ

Food Photo of The Month

Caption: Introducing the September Food Photo of The Month! This amazing photo was taken by our lovely customer [insert name here] and features our signature [insert dish here].

—

The last day of the month is a great time to feature a beautiful photo taken by one of your customers!

OCTOBER 1ST

New Month New Food

Caption: Happy October! As we like to say.. New month, new food! Check out our recently added [insert name of dish here]

-

Use this as an opportunity to show off your newly added dishes on your menu.

OCTOBER 2ND

Featured Special of The Week

Do This: Every week showcase your featured special of the week alongside a mouth-watering photo of the dish.

–

Use this as an opportunity to showcase a popular dish that you are proud of and emphasize that it is only available this week to encourage your followers to come try it.

OCTOBER 3RD

Quote
Share this: "Love at first bite."
– Unknown

–

Creative use of a quote can help you drive more engagement and shares towards your restaurant. Branding relevant quotes with your logo on them will help expand your restaurants digital footprint.

OCTOBER 4TH

Feature Regular Customers

Do This: Give a shoutout to one of your regular customers and have them share a quick story or what their favorite dish is!

—

Show appreciation to those who support you and your business day in and day out!

OCTOBER 5TH

Highlighting a Review

Caption: I'm always grateful for the incredible reviews our customers leave us. Thank you [name of customer]!

—

Reviews are arguably the most important part of a successful restaurant. Make sure to share and showcase those hard-earned stars across your social media platforms. Not only will this entice potential clients, but it will encourage previous clients to also leave kind remarks.

OCTOBER 6TH

National Coffee with a Cop Day

Do This: Host a Coffee with a Cop Day event at your restaurant to show your support for local law enforcement!

—

This day, celebrated annually on October 6th is "a day dedicated to encourage communication and positive interactions between law enforcement agencies and the public." (according to coffeewithacop.com)

OCTOBER 7TH

Local Events

Do this: Share photos from a local event you attended or hosted!

—

Showing that you are involved in your community and attend town events is appealing to potential customers.

OCTOBER 8TH

This or That

Do This: Showcase two popular entrees and have your followers choose which they would rather have!

—

'This or that' is an amazing conversation starter!

OCTOBER 9TH

Share a Customers Photo

Do This: Share a customer's photo that they posted on social media. Make sure to tag them and show your appreciation for them sharing their meal with the internet!

–

Word of mouth is the most powerful marketing tool. Sharing other customer photos will encourage others to share their photos online!

OCTOBER 10TH

Featured Special of The Week

Do This: Every week showcase your featured special of the week alongside a mouth-watering photo of the dish.

—

Use this as an opportunity to showcase a popular dish that you are proud of and emphasize that it is only available this week to encourage your followers to come try it.

OCTOBER 11TH

Events

Do this: Create a post letting your audience know that you have availability for private events!

—

Whether you have private event space or a birthday party package – make sure to let your social media followers know!

OCTOBER 12TH

The Most Delicious Gift

Share this: Did you know we offer gift cards? Stop by during business hours or give us a call at 888-888-8888 to purchase one.

—

Let your followers know that you have gift certificates available for purchase!

OCTOBER 12TH

Relax and Socialize

Caption: Realize and socialize tonight with your friends at [insert restaurant name]!

-

Share this along with a photo of your atmosphere to get your followers excited!

OCTOBER 13TH

Grab N' Go

Do This: Consider creating a limited amount of grab n' go meals for those who don't have time to order ahead and just want to stop by on their way home from work.

—

Share this on your social media's a few hours prior to dinner and see what the response is!

OCTOBER 14TH

National Dessert Day

Do This: Share a photo of a dessert and use the hashtag #NationalDessertDay!

–

If you are feeling extra generous run a promotion for a free dessert with any purchase of an entrée today only.

OCTOBER 15TH

Loyalty Program

Do This: Consider launching a social media loyalty program where customers can earn points for dining and sharing photos of their food online!

—

Getting customers into a restaurant is the first step in building a successful restaurant. The harder part is keeping customers coming back consistently. This is exactly where a loyalty program comes in! It gives customers an incentive to keep coming back.

OCTOBER 16TH

Showcase Some Behind the Scenes Content

Do This: Share a photo or a video showcasing the behind the scenes of your restaurant.

–

Whether this is showing your employees getting ready for a busy night or your chef preparing the food, social media loves to see the behind the scenes.

OCTOBER 17TH

Most Popular Plate

Caption: Tonight's most popular plate was the [insert name of dish here]. [Add a more in-depth description here]!

-

Keep your followers informed on what's trending on your menu!

OCTOBER 18ᵀᴴ

Featured Special of The Week

Do This: Every week showcase your featured special of the week alongside a mouth-watering photo of the dish.

—

Use this as an opportunity to showcase a popular dish that you are proud of and emphasize that it is only available this week to encourage your followers to come try it.

OCTOBER 19TH

Tweet

Do This: Find a viral foodie tweet (or use one of your own) and repost it to your other platforms.

—

Whether this is sharing a meme or restaurant fun fact it's a new and engaging way to do so.

OCTOBER 20TH

We'll Bring the Food to You

Do This: Share/create a graphic that shows all the ways to get your restaurants food delivered.

—

Nowadays there are so many different food delivery services! Showcase all the ones where you can order your restaurant on!

OCTOBER 21ST

Get to Know Your Customers Day

Caption: It's Get to Know Your Customers Day! Would love to get to know more of you. Anyone interested in stopping by for a cup of coffee this week?

–

Coffee networking is a great way to meet new people in your local community.

OCTOBER 22ND

Appetizer or Dessert

Caption: If you had to choose, would you rather have [insert most popular appetizer] or [insert most popular dessert]?

–

I know choosing both would be the ideal option but showcase some of your most popular dishes with this fun competition. Not only will this show off your delicious food, but it will also encourage followers to engage on the post.

OCTOBER 23RD

Quote

Share this: "Part of the secret of a success in life is to eat what you like and let the food fight it out inside." - Mark Twain

–

Creative use of a quote can help you drive more engagement and shares towards your restaurant. Branding relevant quotes with your logo on them will help expand your restaurants digital footprint.

OCTOBER 24ᵀᴴ

Cooking Class

Do this: Host a cooking class with your chef and teach locals how to make some of your most popular dishes!

–

If you don't have the space in your restaurant host a class online via a video conference.

OCTOBER 25TH

This or That

Do This: Showcase two popular entrees and have your followers choose which they would rather have!

–

'This or that' is an amazing conversation starter!

OCTOBER 26TH

Featured Special of The Week

Do This: Every week showcase your featured special of the week alongside a mouth-watering photo of the dish.

—

Use this as an opportunity to showcase a popular dish that you are proud of and emphasize that it is only available this week to encourage your followers to come try it.

OCTOBER 27TH

Highlighting a Review

Caption: I'm always grateful for the incredible review's customers leave us. Thank you [name of client]!

—

Reviews are arguably the most important part of a successful restaurant. Make sure to share and showcase those hard-earned stars across your social media platforms. Not only will this entice potential clients, but it will encourage previous clients to also leave kind remarks.

OCTOBER 28TH

FAQ

Do This: Answer some commonly asked questions about your food, hours, delivery etc.

–

If you are constantly getting calls or emails about a certain question, save yourself some time and answer it on social media!

OCTOBER 29TH

Share a Recipe

Do This: Share a recipe of one of your dishes with your audience!

—

Contrary to popular belief, sharing recipes for some of your dishes does not diminish your brand value. Recipes deepen the bond between your food and your clientele and prove your expertise even more.

OCTOBER 30TH

Things To Do This Weekend
Caption: Share a list of local events or something fun to do this weekend!

-

Use this post to showcase your sense of community.

OCTOBER 31ST

Food Photo of The Month

Caption: Introducing the October Food Photo of The Month! This amazing photo was taken by our lovely customer [insert name here] and features our signature [insert dish here].

–

The last day of the month is a great time to feature a beautiful photo taken by one of your customers!

NOVEMBER 1ST

New Month New Food

Caption: Happy November! As we like to say.. New month, new food! Check out our recently added [insert name of dish here]

—

Use this as an opportunity to show off your newly added dishes on your menu.

NOVEMBER 2ND

Win a Table for 2

Do This: Give away a table for 2 on the house. Have followers enter by tagging three friends in the comments!

—

Also – make sure to mention that they must be following your account to be eligible to win! This is a great way to attract new eyes to your page!

NOVEMBER 3ᴿᴰ

Featured Special of The Week

Do This: Every week showcase your featured special of the week alongside a mouth-watering photo of the dish.

–

Use this as an opportunity to showcase a popular dish that you are proud of and emphasize that it is only available this week to encourage your followers to come try it.

NOVEMBER 4TH

All Smiles Here

Do This: Take a photo of some happy diners enjoying their food and share it on your socials!

—

Make sure to ask for permission before taking the photo and ensure that they are okay with it being posted online.

NOVEMBER 5TH

Gotta Love Memes

Do This: Find a funny food related meme to share with your audience. A good laugh can never hurt!

—

Who doesn't like a funny meme?

NOVEMBER 6TH

Daylight Saving Time Ends Tomorrow

Do This: Remind your followers that Daylight savings ends tomorrow

—

Reminder: Clocks are turned backward 1 hour!

NOVEMBER 7TH

Food Blogger

Do this: Invite a local food blogger with a social media presence to eat at your restaurant for free!

—

In today's culture, one viral post from a well-known foodie can blow up your restaurant.

NOVEMBER 8TH

Online Orders

Do This: Encourage people to order online with a post walking them through how easy it is to order on your website!

—

In this digital era we are living in, it's becoming more and more prominent for takeout orders to be ordered online. Make a post encouraging people to do so as it will save your employees tons of time from over-the-phone orders.

NOVEMBER 8TH

Highlighting a Review

Caption: Thank you for your kind words [Name of customer who shared the review]! Incredibly thankful for reviews like this.

—

Reviews are arguably the most important part of a successful restaurant. Make sure to share and showcase those hard-earned stars across your social media platforms. Not only will this entice potential clients, but it will encourage previous clients to also leave kind remarks.

NOVEMBER 9TH

One Thing

Caption: If you could only eat one thing for the rest of your life, what would it be?

—

Well, this will be interesting!

NOVEMBER 10TH

Quote

Share this: "Food Is the ingredient that binds us together" – Unknown

–

Creative use of a quote can help you drive more engagement and shares towards your restaurant. Branding relevant quotes with your logo on them will help expand your restaurants digital footprint.

NOVEMBER 11TH

Veterans Day

Caption: Happy Veterans Day. Thank you to all our military personnel for your service and sacrifices.

—

Today is a day to honor military veterans and all who have served in the United States Armed Forces.

NOVEMBER 12ᵀᴴ

Featured Special of The Week

Do This: Every week showcase your featured special of the week alongside a mouth-watering photo of the dish.

–

Use this as an opportunity to showcase a popular dish that you are proud of and emphasize that it is only available this week to encourage your followers to come try it.

NOVEMBER 13TH

World Kindness Day

Caption: It's World Kindness Day. Spread kindness every day but especially today.

—

World Kindness Day is a holiday that promotes the importance of spreading kindness amongst all.

NOVEMBER 14TH

Signature Dish

Do This: Showcase a heavenly photo of one of your signature dishes!

—

In the restaurant business – the quality of your photos of social media goes a long way. Make sure to study up on some camera tips or hire a professional photographer to shoot your food.

NOVEMBER 15TH

Tapas Night

Do This: Host a tapas night where customers can order a bunch of mini appetizers instead of one entrée.

—

A tapa is an appetizer in Spanish cuisine.

NOVEMBER 16TH

Brunch

Do This: Encourage followers to stop by for brunch! Showcase a beautifully plated brunch special along with a descriptive caption.

-

Consider offering a 2 for $XX deal for brunch on slow days!

NOVEMBER 17TH

Happy Hour

Do This: Create a happy hour special. Share the details along with some photos of your refreshing drinks.

—

Having a happy hour is an excellent way to increase foot traffic and sales during the slower parts of the day.

NOVEMBER 18TH

Did you know...

Do This: Share a fun fact about your food or your restaurant that most of your followers wouldn't know!

—

Believe it or not, people love to know the story behind a restaurant.

NOVEMBER 19TH

½ Price Drinks Today!

Do this: Offer half price drinks to get people in the door!

—

Having a special promotion is a great way to attract new people to your restaurant!

NOVEMBER 20TH

Take Out Special

Do This: Offer an exclusive take out special for those who follow you on social media!

—

Use this as an opportunity to showcase some of the benefits to following you on social media!

NOVEMBER 21ST

Featured Special of The Week
Do This: Every week showcase your featured special of the week alongside a mouth-watering photo of the dish.

–

Use this as an opportunity to showcase a popular dish that you are proud of and emphasize that it is only available this week to encourage your followers to come try it.

NOVEMBER 22ND

Share a Customers Photo

Do This: Share a customer's photo that they posted on social media. Make sure to tag them and show your appreciation for them sharing their meal with the internet!

–

Word of mouth is the most powerful marketing tool. Sharing other customer photos will encourage others to share their photos online!

NOVEMBER 23RD

National Espresso Day
Caption: It's National Espresso Day! Would love to meet more of you. Feel free to stop by today for an espresso on the house!

—

Coffee networking is a great way to meet new people in your local community.

NOVEMBER 24TH

Staff Bio

Do This: Share a short blurb about one of your employees alongside a photo of them!

—

Share their role at your restaurant along with anything they want to share about their life outside of work. Some examples are hobbies, family members, favorite food, etc.

NOVEMBER 25TH

Feature Regular Customers

Do This: Give a shoutout to one of your regular customers and have them share a quick story or what their favorite dish is!

—

Show appreciation to those who support you and your business day in and day out!

NOVEMBER 25TH

Introduce a New Dessert

Caption: Introduce a newly added dessert item with an HD photo!

–

Keep your menu and your socials fresh with a delicious new dessert item!

NOVEMBER 26TH

This or That

Do This: Showcase two popular entrees and have your followers choose which they would rather have!

–

'This or that' is an amazing conversation starter!

NOVEMBER 27TH

Statistics

Do This: Share a statistic that emphasize the locality of your restaurant!

—

For Example: Did you know our food was rated in the top 10 restaurants in our city last year?

Or

Did you know our downtown was rated as the one of the top 10 downtowns in New Jersey for dining?

NOVEMBER 28TH

Featured Special of The Week

Do This: Every week showcase your featured special of the week alongside a mouth-watering photo of the dish.

—

Use this as an opportunity to showcase a popular dish that you are proud of and emphasize that it is only available this week to encourage your followers to come try it.

NOVEMBER 29TH

Things To Do This Weekend
Caption: Share a list of local events or something fun to do this weekend!

–

Use this post to showcase your sense of community.

NOVEMBER 30TH

Food Photo of The Month

Caption: Introducing the November Food Photo of The Month! This amazing photo was taken by our lovely customer [insert name here] and features our signature [insert dish here].

—

The last day of the month is a great time to feature a beautiful photo taken by one of your customers!

DECEMBER 1ST

New Month New Food

Caption: Happy December! As we like to say.. New month, new food! Check out our recently added [insert name of dish here]

-

Use this as an opportunity to show off your newly added dishes on your menu.

DECEMBER 2ND

Food Wars

Do This: Showcase two photos of different dishes and have your audience choose which they would rather have.

—

This is an excellent way to get your followers to engage with your content

DECEMBER 3RD

Reminder

Do This: Remind your followers that you have reservation availability tonight!

-

This is a great way to initiate a conversation with a potential buyer!

DECEMBER 4TH

To Do List

Do This: Make a creative to do list featuring a visit at your restaurant!

—

To do:
→ Go to [insert restaurant]
→ Have a margarita
→ Hang out by the fire pit

DECEMBER 5ᵀᴴ

What Everyone is Saying

Do This: Share some main points from reviews you have received recently.

—

Example: "BEST seafood ever!" "We are addicted to this place" "Their burgers are the best in New York'

DECEMBER 6TH

Featured Special of The Week

Do This: Every week showcase your featured special of the week alongside a mouth-watering photo of the dish.

–

Use this as an opportunity to showcase a popular dish that you are proud of and emphasize that it is only available this week to encourage your followers to come try it.

DECEMBER 7TH

Customer Spotlight

Caption: Meet our amazing customers, [insert details about your client here]. Thank you for dining with us at [insert restaurant name here].

-

Highlighting and empowering your customers is extremely touching and a great way to show your appreciation for their business.

DECEMBER 8TH

National Brownie Day

Do This: Celebrate National Brownie Day by creating a special brownie dessert!

—

National Brownie Day celebrated annually on December 8th.

DECEMBER 9TH

Upcoming Local Events

Do This: Share some local events with your followers. It's important to emphasize the sense of community within your town.

–

If you feel inclined – host an event of your own at your restaurant.

DECEMBER 10TH

Share a Local Article

Do This: Share a relevant article about your community. Whether it's about an upcoming event or an interesting story share it amongst your social media audience.

–

Sharing local articles will show your support and involvement in your community.

DECEMBER 11TH

Quote

Share this: "Not all relationships will lead to marriage, some will help you discover new restaurants." - Unknown

–

Creative use of a quote can help you drive more engagement and shares towards your restaurant. Branding relevant quotes with your logo on them will help expand your restaurants digital footprint.

DECEMBER 12TH

Highlighting a Review

Caption: It made me feel so good to hear these reviews from these amazing customers!

—

Reviews are arguably the most important part of a successful restaurant. Make sure to share and showcase those hard-earned stars across your social media platforms. Not only will this entice potential clients, but it will encourage previous clients to also leave kind remarks.

DECEMBER 13TH

Zeitgeist

Do This: Share something in the zeitgeist that relates to food trends.

—

Staying relevant with all the latest food trends is key as a restaurant owner.

DECEMBER 14TH

Featured Special of The Week

Do This: Every week showcase your featured special of the week alongside a mouth-watering photo of the dish.

—

Use this as an opportunity to showcase a popular dish that you are proud of and emphasize that it is only available this week to encourage your followers to come try it.

DECEMBER 15TH

Off-The-Menu Special
Do This: Create a special exclusively for your social media fans.

—

This will make customers feel like they have access to something special by following your online!

DECEMBER 16TH

Give Customers an Incentive to Post a Photo of Their Food

Do This: Incentivize food photo sharing by giving away a gift card to one lucky customer who shares a photo of their meal with #YourRestaurant.

–

Having customers share their food online is an excellent way to reach an entirely new audience.

DECEMBER 17TH

Employment Opportunities

Do This: Ever have trouble hiring new employees? Post a flyer with details of the positions you are looking to fill.

—

Social media is a great place to spread the word about job offerings. Use local hashtags to make sure you hit the right audience!

DECEMBER 18TH

Kid-friendly

Do This: Share a quick snapshot of some of the meals on your kid's menu.

–

This post will give parents with picky eaters a sigh of relief!

DECEMBER 19TH

Movie Tickets

Do This: Host a giveaway for two movie tickets to your local theater. Use this as an opportunity to support local businesses and promote your services at the same time.

—

Implement rules to enter such as they must be following you and tag 3 friends in the comments. People love free stuff!

DECEMBER 20TH

Featured Special of The Week

Do This: Every week showcase your featured special of the week alongside a mouth-watering photo of the dish.

–

Use this as an opportunity to showcase a popular dish that you are proud of and emphasize that it is only available this week to encourage your followers to come try it.

DECEMBER 21ST

On a Diet?

Do This: Share some healthy dishes that you'd recommend those on a diet to order.

—

Make sure to describe the dishes in their entirety and let your followers know why these are a healthier option.

DECEMBER 22ND

Share a Recipe

Do This: Share a recipe of one of your dishes with your audience!

—

Contrary to popular belief, sharing recipes for some of your dishes does not diminish your brand value. Recipes deepen the bond between your food and your clientele and prove your expertise even more.

DECEMBER 23RD

Holiday Lights

Do This: Showcase your restaurant decorated with some holiday's lights!

—

If you have the time, consider creating/sponsoring a holiday lights contest!

DECEMBER 24TH

Christmas Eve

Do This: Wish everyone a wonderful Christmas Eve!

—

Show off some of your holiday decor in your restaurant and around your town.

DECEMBER 25TH

Christmas Day

Caption: Merry Christmas to everyone! Wishing you love, prosperity, happiness, and success!

–

Annual Merry Christmas post!

DECEMBER 26TH

Gotta Love Memes

Do This: Find a funny food related meme to share with your audience. A good laugh can never hurt!

–

Who doesn't like a funny meme?

DECEMBER 27ᵀᴴ

Featured Special of The Week

Do This: Every week showcase your featured special of the week alongside a mouth-watering photo of the dish.

—

Use this as an opportunity to showcase a popular dish that you are proud of and emphasize that it is only available this week to encourage your followers to come try it.

DECEMBER 28TH

FAQ Video

Do This: Record a 1-minute video answering commonly asked questions about your restaurant!

—

Example questions to answer:
Do you accept reservations?
What is your most popular meal?
Do you offer delivery?
What are your hours?

DECEMBER 29TH

Did you know...

Caption: Did you know our [insert dish here] is made from all locally sourced ingredients and is 100% gluten free.

-

Showcase a gluten free meal made with locally sourced ingredients.

DECEMBER 30TH

Food Photo of The Month

Caption: Introducing the December Food Photo of The Month! This amazing photo was taken by our lovely customer [insert name here] and features our signature [insert dish here].

—

The end of the month is a great time to feature a beautiful photo taken by one of your customers!

DECEMBER 31ST

New Year's Eve

Do This: Wish your followers a Happy New Year's Eve!

-

New Year, New Food?

Printed in Great Britain
by Amazon